NEON SOUL

NEON SOUL

—

a collection of poetry and prose

ALEXANDRA ELLE

Andrews McMeel
PUBLISHING®

Lately, I have been longing for something to fill me and light my world on fire again. It's been a struggle. Sometimes the creative process leaves me feeling dull and muted, almost like I have lost my spark. Maybe a piece of my magic, too. When my healing happened, the fire that was burning within me simmered down. I had put in all the work, created and protected a space that was sacred, and established an emotionally safe sanctuary that I built brick by brick. The self-work was a part of my manifestation. What I lost in the process of discovery was the ability to tap into the parts of me that were screaming out for a voice. That voice has been muffled by growth and experience. By unwinding and unbreaking. It's like my senses decided to power off because the darkest parts of me had been healed by the vibrant hues of electrifying truth, shocking resilience, and blinding belonging. Perhaps they figured I didn't need my vibrancy anymore because, well, I had found it. But I do need it because life without neon is dull.

Truthfully, sometimes I worry that I can't grab on to my colors because I am not broken anymore. There's a lingering fear that being whole threatens my creative voice. The hurt happened. And, yes, it

will always be a reminder of what I have been through. Some scars will linger, perhaps even a few memories and remnants of self-doubt will live dormant on a cot in the back of my mind, but I decided that trauma will not be my resting place. Pain and suffering will not make a home out of me. They will not have windows or doors to my soul. And they are no longer allowed to nestle in my space for comfort and refuge. I am not a vessel for parasitic emotions or past times.

Evolution is nearly impossible if leeches of the past are draining the potential and courage to walk in the direction of relief. Sadness and sorrow will not be where I swim or settle. Because if I have learned anything in this life, it's that my healing is what's most valuable. Growth and resilience and the ability to take control of my life from the front seat are what I have worked so hard for.

Although writing this book created an abundance of anxiety for me, I needed it to reignite my spark. There have been lessons in every setback. Coming up with content was a struggle, and I believe it's because a lot has changed for me, in a good way. I am no longer finding my path like I was in my early twenties. I am on it and walking intentionally in love, light, and my lifework. Living isn't as rattled by disappointment, chaos, and emotional longing anymore. It's slowed down. I've found peace. And most of all I am happy. I feared that my contentment wasn't what people wanted to read about. In my mind, I assumed more eyes would be looking for the pain to relate to. Not the joy. Or perhaps they'd be searching for the fear and not the possibility of goodness coming to fruition. Because who wants to read about happiness when they are still in the thick of aching and turmoil? Nevertheless, I hope whoever is reading this wants a different view and perspective. A different angle on life after the bad and all right morph into fulfilling self-celebration, because preparing for joy is just as important as healing from hurt.

neon soul

lava hisses from
my soul like ash
and neon.
hot and bold
and colorful
i unfold into
a dance that
can birth sunlight
and dim darkness.

escape

for every woman
who has been crushed
by love that couldn't love
her:

sometimes you'll
be too magical to contain
in a human heart.

impossible

how are you not
enough?
that is never so.
that can never be.

freedom

give your truth
wings.
let it go.
let it fly.

loss

the question is as hard as
swallowing rocks and as
brutal as stormy waters
crashing to shore.

the question is not always why,
but how do we let go without
falling apart——without crumbling
from loosening our grip on what
was and what could have been.

reminiscent of

love poems that look like
blush lace on brown skin—

that feel like silk.

love poems that shift
and shape broken hearts
back together—

that feel like hope
and look like growth.

love poems that feel
like autumn hugs and
summer warmth.

that sound like prayers and
hymns from ancestors and
grassroots.

love poems that make you
believe in love again.

whole

some people want us at our
worst, shattered and
clumsy
in pieces

dizzied and stumbling
headfirst over heels.

and then some want us
whole.

in one entity, not in
shambles
or ruins but as we are in
our entirety.

unravel

giving my heart a
rest has been nice.

less dizzying.
more delightful.

as i take off my
clothes my skin
remembers to
breathe for once.

the hairs raise from
my arms and seemingly
exhale with the wind
that is rushing through
my cracked window.

slowly i am unraveling.

flight

to feel, to flee.
they exist in the
same body, in the
same heart.

the thrill must be to
conquer my world and
then abandon it—

because what is the fun
of playing when the war
is over.

love lines

like marble or reflections
of the sun dancing on
moonlit water.

stretched skin.
resilient skin.

you tell stories
of growth and spurts
and unsummoned beauty,
because god and matter
made us malleable.

soft like
lips to skin and
blood to bone.

bad timing

my tongue is jumbled
inside of my mouth.
caught in the back
of my throat.

what to say?
how to uncurl?
when you love
someone who doesn't
know—who doesn't
love you.

i can't wash it down.
so the love i have buried
inside me for you just
lingers there with no
direction or plea—
just patience.

the ritual of healing

bathe.
soak.
scrub with
sugar and salt.
wash your hair.
cleanse your body.
taste your tears.
what used to be
is gone now.
what used to be
is no longer yours
to keep.
watch it twirl
down the drain.
watch it dance
away with soot
and skin.
the pain.
the pain.
the pain.

free it.
admit it.
honor it.

gather yourself
drenched in truth.

and let it go.

mess

how dare you
break into pieces
for those who
refuse to help
undo the damage.
who wouldn't even
think to put you
back together,
time and time
again.

submit

all of my instincts want
to collapse and fall into
you, headfirst and with no
fear.

uncomfortable

when you are not
yourself who are you
trying to be?
what disguise
do you fold into
to fit molds and
boxes that do not
belong to you?
you cannot be
happy when in
heaps of yourself,
can you?

push away

i distort my words
to say things that
look like everything
but love.

passage

there's no need to circumnavigate
the journey at hand or ahead.

the growth, the change, the path.

the winds, the twists, the turns.
you will always find a way home.

finale

where can i put us after
we end? how can i fit
you into my life after
we've outgrown the love
we built?

my drawers are full
of everything we couldn't
get to.

there is no more room
to put what we left undone
and unfinished.

upbringing

i never quite belonged
or knew where i came
from.

come from.

belong to.

love didn't show up
too often in my mama's
house.

boundaries

why do you let them
make homes in you
when all they do is
destroy what you've
worked so hard to build?

why do they reign?
who is your ruler, darling?

it's like you have forgotten
you're not empty and that
you are allowed to build
unbreakable things.

you have permission
to mold moats and
descend drawbridges,
form fences and gates made of
steel.

you are allowed to keep
a destruction-free zone
that glimmers and holds
peace of mind, heart, and soul.

you reign, darling.
you are your own home.

self-forgiveness

will you ever forgive yourself
for what you didn't do?
who you didn't love or
let love you?
will you ever be soft
enough on yourself
to be free?

mercy

there is a place in the
past where i left my suffering
and found myself at my own
feet.

flowers

you can only start where you are.
mistakes are water——grow your
lessons from them.

swallow falls

god lives here.
there is proof
in the sound
of water on rocks.
trees swirling their
leaves in the wind.
angels are singing.

hitchhiker

pain had caught a ride on
my back for way too long.
i decided to drop it
off and leave it stranded
on the side of the road.
letting go is a choice,
and i will not look back.

tears

sometimes water takes refuge in
places where it cannot flow.
it puddles and becomes stagnant
when it really needs to
be free.
but what happens when it collects
in one place?
maybe oceans will form.
or perhaps, when i overflow
from my eyes, god will send
my water over the edge of my
heart and create falling glory.

daring

to write means to be honest,
to expose your deepest truth
and passion and fear.
you don't have to make
sense. spill your soul
anyway.

bold

if you refuse to love yourself
the way you should be loved
you will always be searching
for something to flood your
emptiness.

along the way

the voyage home required
getting lost and falling
into bunkers that trapped me
and refused to open.
i would've done anything
to find myself sooner—
if i could keep the lessons,
too.

grip

trust yourself enough to
let go when you feel
your hands unfold.

unseen

and even when no one
is looking, love yourself.

pieces

i have left behind
pieces of me on
the sleeves of shirts
that didn't belong
in my wardrobe.

bits of heart,
soul, and bone.

remnants of sugar
and sweetness that
couldn't be swallowed or
stomached.

i was cleaning up mess
after mess because the
floor got too slippery to
stand on.

broken dishes
left welts on more than
just my hands.

and still, i stand.

fill

when you're a giver
it's hard to remember
that you must contribute
and pour into your
well-being, too.

hands

nana used to sit me on the step
that separated her dining and
living room to comb my
thick cottony hair.
part after part.
plait after plait.
we would settle down
into our seat as she created
magic with her hands.
they always struck
me as the strongest hands
in the world.
she cooked with them.
cleaned with them.
calmed babies and big
kids with hugs and swaddles.
her resilience shone through
her palms like the sun through
parting clouds,
and they were still kind enough
to tame a mountain of hair
without force.

her grip, as she curated twists and
turns, braids and beads, was gentle.
i would fall asleep there to the rhythm
of each step.

part.
grease.
brush.
braid.

and wake up thinking
how nana's hands were
the softest hands in the world.

the unlearning

who taught you not
to give to yourself,
that loving yourself
first was a sin?
and how will you
unlearn the destructiveness
of filling them to the brim
when your cup is bone-dry
and paper-thin?

belong

when something is for you
it will not run or hide or
avoid being yours.

brainwashed

who taught you to unlove
yourself the way you did
so perfectly?

through and through

i have learned to
forgive myself
and through that i
have mastered
survival.

unconditional

fill where you are empty with
love, love, and more love.
even when you feel love itself
isn't enough.

shame

when i learned that shaming
my journey was creating a voice
that wouldn't speak up
i discovered why i'd been
quiet all these years.

victim

be honest, they say.
tell us what happened
that day.

tell us who took your
soul and cut out your
tongue.

did you look while
they snatched the best
parts of you?

did you like it?
you must've.

please, tell us why
you let them.

the one

there will be so many—
or maybe a few . . .
who won't ever love you.
and then there will be one
who will.

rebirth

there will be moments when
you will bloom fully and then
wilt, only to bloom again.
if we can learn anything from
flowers it is that resilience is born
even when we feel like we are
dying.

loose grip

i have outstretched who i am
like a fitted sheet trying to
hug a bed too wide
to excuse who you are.
each and every time i protect
you.
and each and every time
you let go.

stray

finding yourself never looks
the same. it tastes different each time
you stray. the journey back will
always be rewarding. home always
feels as good as it sounds.

uprising

i thought that
i would never grow
again. that you had
taken the best parts
of me and swallowed
the key. until one day
it happened and i was
free.

joy

your joy is not to be
understood or examined.
questioned or doubted.
it is to be invited in
and celebrated.
it is to be given
space to roam and
flow in and out of
your soul.

clueless

i remember loving you so hard that i nearly
broke in half and collapsed into a pile of dust.

you were my first everything and nothing packaged
in perfection, drenched in one-sided dedication.

i had no clue what i was doing.
hearts are not like hands. two isn't
better than one when the other is broken.

i'd never felt what i felt when we collided.
and each time we did, i broke my heart like it
lived on my sleeve and not behind a cage of protection.

then i remember unloving you and how it was
magical and how i grew wings that day because
enough was finally enough.

thick with unlearning and taut with restitching
the opened wounds. i was finally free.

love doesn't look like the picture i painted.
love never looked like us.

fine

the worst lie i have ever told myself—
and there have been many—is i am fine,
as if it were a sin to admit that i wasn't.
as if the sea would rise above me and absorb
into the clouds to replace the tears that i wasn't
honest enough to shed.
i'm fine left gaping holes in my neon soul and
enabled men to come and go freely as they wished.
i'm fine left me lonely and unwell—
until one day i decided to tell the truth.

daily

the best way to love
yourself is to do it daily.
not in shame or in secret,
but out loud for the birds to hear
and ocean to feel.

best friend

link your hands
and settle into yourself.

you are allowed to be your
own comfort, your own friend.

reward

you loving yourself
opens up windows and
doors that can never be
closed by outsiders without
permission.

healing

there are bits of you
that you'll never get
back, and that is what
will make you whole.

resilience practice

look yourself in the eye
when you feel the most
hurt, the most ashamed
and unworthy.

when you are barely
able to stand up
straight because the
pain runs deeper
than you are willing
to go.

and love yourself
entirely anyway.

sixteen-year-old self

loving does not require
losing you yourself.
it is not a ticket to
self-destruction.
you do not have
to become a martyr or
a maid.
loving does not require
you to shut up and sit down.
it will not leave you quiet
or feeling naked when
fully clothed or abandoned
in your own body.
love does not require
you to misplace your
map or directions
or identity—
it is not permission
to lose your way home.

balance

you can be soft and still be sturdy.
you can be a force and still be delicate.

bloom

plant your pain in
pockets of sun-warmed
soil.

let it sprout and
come to life.

allow it space to
grow and bloom.

then cut the sorrow
and suffering, angst
and agony, stem by
stem from your garden.

place them in a vase in
copper-kissed water on
your dining room table,
right in the middle of mess and
madness.

and enjoy the beauty that
comes from grit and growth.

the truth

love commands
embracing the
moments that
turn your fear
into faith and
vulnerability
into victory.
that molds
your imperfections
into beauty and
emptiness into
abundance.
love requires
your doubt
so it can show
you how much
louder it is than
any lie your mind
can make up.

death

when i return to the earth
i pray to bring joy and peace
with me.

i look to leave behind bookshelves
of books and hearts filled to the
brim with tenderness.

when i return to the earth
i pray the transition is easy
and soft.

student

the hardest thing
about unlearning
is letting go of what
you thought you
knew.

refuge

where do you go when the world
is too loud

and the thick of the air
is too heavy to move
through?

how do you find peace

and where does it feel good?

fools have wings

you are not foolish for falling.
how else will you learn to
fly?

whole

in or out of love,
with or without
a whole heart or
a half,
i am still complete.

real love

i've never had anyone say to me that love,
real love, would be my greatest joy.
that it would come in the night
and seep into my heart like spilled
milk into the cracks of reclaimed
wood tables.

no one ever said love should be safe
or feel sacred or that it's better when
shared with two whole hearts instead
of halves.

autumn

when i drove away from you
autumn had just shown up
with all her beauty and glory
and crisp recollection of shift
and submission.
how fitting.
a season of change
and death and rebirth.

i was alone for the first
time in a long while,
and my journey away
had been waiting for me,
without you, with arms
opened like tree branches
and applause from clapping
leaves that had been set on
fire by the sun.

when i drove away from you
with nothing but my heart
on my sleeve and the ocean
in my eyes the whole world
opened up like parting skies
and blooming belonging that'd
been begging to be free.

i was alone for the first time
in a long while, and the voyage
back home looked like
the love i'd been waiting for.

bogeyman

i do not have lessons from him
about how men should love women.

how men should treat women.

instead, in my suitcases and
duffel bags i have packed away that women don't
exist until a man enters and exits and
turns her life into a messy home and kitchen
into slave quarters and bedrooms into
dungeons.

i do not have lessons from him
about how fathers should teach
daughters.

how fathers should love daughters.

but i do carry with me in my knapsack
and shoulder bag lessons that save my
daughters from men like him.

how to birth a lesson

whatever and
whoever
that we love
and lose becomes
a star in our darkest
sky.
some may even
become moons.

evolution

feel. heal. grow.
that alone is
an act of rebellion.

explore. love. change.
that alone can lead
to triumph.

one-sided

you will love people
who will never love you
back. and still you mustn't
ever misplace your magic.

language

your hurt
doesn't have
to speak for
your heart.

the journey to paper

poetry is birthed from
pain and love meeting
somewhere in the middle.

someplace between the
towns of hurt and cities of
healing.

love and loneliness live
there, too.

poetry is explored through
the salt of tears and howls
to the moon from the heart.

not for you

if it feels forced,
free it.

self-love

and if love is something
you are missing, you are
not looking hard enough
or deep enough, love.

beautiful girl

being called beautiful
won't be enough for her.

it won't make her crumble
at their feet. she will not
be in ruins on the rugs of
their bedroom floors.

because so many others
are beautiful, too, but
she will always be so
much more.

origin

in love and okay.
in love and whole.
in love and safe.

i did not know i am
where love lived all
this time.

you

you are like the springtime to me.
the more you love, the
more you bloom.
the warmer it gets, the more
beautiful you become.

revelation

loving your entire
self is like finding a
rare gem in your
back pocket.
you won't always
know where it
will come from,
or when it will arrive,
but when it does
cherish it, hold it,
keep it close.

miscarriage

i am trying not to be angry
with my body for this.

but who says

let me give you the sun

just to extinguish it upon receipt?

vigorous

it won't always make
sense but it should
always make you feel
alive.

opened door

the way you left scared me—
but how i could think to let
you back in scared me even
more.

ability

you can because the birds
sing in the morning.

and because the sun hasn't yet
risen.

you can because the moon shines
brightly without a reminder to show
up and beam down.

uneasy

i may not always be the easiest
woman to love.

but i love hard enough
to collapse the sky.

strong enough to hold together
crumbling mountains.

and deep enough to drown the sea.

from rejection

my womanhood was constructed
plank by plank from the love of self,
not the love of man.

learning alone

in order to undo something
you must first render yourself
hopeless to regain hope.
you must journey alone
to outgrow the tall tales of
loneliness.

you are not lonely.
you are healing.

and healing takes
learning, all by
yourself.

write

give your words a home
on paper.

build them up.

create their lives
as you see fit.

husband

with my eyes closed i
can trace your every move.

without touching you i can feel
your love pressed against mine.

resilience

look at you.
still standing
after being
knocked down
and thrown out.

look at you.
still growing
after being
picked and plucked
and prodded out of
your home.

look at you.
still dancing
and singing
after being
defeated and
disassembled.

look at you, love.
still here and hopeful
after it all.

stay

when they leave
do not follow them.

there is no need
to chase what is
running away from
you.

rescue

because saying *no*
will sometimes be
the thing that saves
your soul.

linger

we can't always unlove them.
some will linger and stay with
us long after the sun burns out.
long after the moon loses its
shimmering glow.

freedom

dance and be free.
leap and fly and
roam with wonder.

find joy in the little
things that cost you
nothing.

survive

when you sit back and
dream your life dreams
do they seem real to you?

can you touch them?
taste them?

do you love them
wholly and truly without
regret or second thought?

can you still feel them when
others refuse to let them land
on earth to grow?

will they survive the
doubt when you give
them permission to be
born?

wholeness

the question should always be,
when you're feeling half yourself,

when you're not whole with someone
in your ear and by your side,

who are you without them?

past life

past lives create future poems
and love songs and memories
that thrive long after we die.

they give hope to the hopeless
and warmth to the frigid hearts
too scared to love again.

past lives remind us that what
we don't want is behind us
and what we do is within reach.

phoenix

if you're able enough
to descend and crash
from what hurts and crushes
your soul into pieces

you are just as able
to climb out of the
fiery madness and soar
again.

uncover

being okay is sometimes
the scariest part because
then we have no place to
hide our fear.

the difference

when i fell in love
and it didn't hurt
or threaten my joy
i knew it was finally
real and safe enough
to stand in.

credence

trust yourself enough
to let go and live even
when it's the most
uncomfortable thing
to bear.

enjoy

don't forget to stop
and see and listen
and love. because
one day this will
all be gone and so
will we.

enjoy the journey

the best part of not knowing
is learning how to get there
and getting lost along the way.

step by step

we often find our way by
getting lost and found,
time and time again.
by breaking and unbreaking
piece by peace, one by one.
by unlearning and relearning.
by shifting and shaping into
who we are in this imperfect
and uncertain life.

certainly

your confidence doesn't have
to be dressed in their doubt.

blind

you are certainly the most beautiful
being this earth has ever had the pleasure
of hosting.

i just wish you knew what i knew.
see what i see.

masterpiece

it feels good to feel whole. to not live in pieces or in fear.
it feels nice to belong to myself. to be enthralled with the
endless possibilities to find who i am. we are often too confused
about what parts of us deserve to stay in our loud and vibrant lives,
but why is that? when all of the mess can make a magnificent
masterpiece.

gentleness

as you hunt for who you are
in the thick of this life—
as you trample and fall
in fields of failure and regret—
promise yourself one thing:
that you will be gentle and
offer up grace when you need
it. because there is enough suffering
in the world for you not to be soft
with the shell and soul that carries you.

flow

water carries and cleanses.
let us learn life lessons from
its ability to flow freely, even
through the thick of it.

light

no matter the darkness
light always finds a way
to seep in and bring refuge.

when hearts break

at first it will hurt.
it will make you
sick every time
you remember
the pain or the
absence or
the longing.
and for months
it might eat at you.
perhaps it will devour
you and drown you in
tears and turmoil.

but then one day it won't.
that day alone will remind
you of how malleable the heart
is, even through destruction.

homage

remembering doesn't
always mean to relive.
sometimes it is simply
a reminder to give yourself
thanks for making it out alive.

tutorial

learning how to unlove you
was the very best part.

some is not all

some will love your art.

they will keep coming back for
spoonfuls with full bellies and
empty plates—begging for more.

some will not.

they will pick at and dissect and reject
everything good that you thought to offer.
be content with both.

both the light and dark
assist in discovering
the neon of your soul.

creation

in the thick of
cream and sugar—
right in the middle
of sweetness and
soft—there is the center
of the universe.
and it crafted me carefully
from diamond powder
and rust.

regret

i would love nothing more
than to close doors that were
opened for men who shouldn't
have been welcomed.

soul

soft and ripe
like figs in full bloom,
mild and delicious and
sweet.

more than more (ode to my daughter)

i love you more than the moon
loves the sky—
than the sun loves gently setting
on the west.

i love you more than the universe adores
its galaxies—
than the stars love dancing
in the darkness.

i love you more than all things good.

you are the most incredible thing
that could have happened to my heart.

vows

grow with me in
joy and pain,
hopes and dreams,
highs and lows,
happiness and madness.

bloom with me through
thick and thin,
better or worse,
certainty and fear.

journey with me
hand in hand.

adore with me
heart to heart.

create art with me.
create gardens with me.
create deep oceans and vast
sands.

bring to being yourself with me.
and in the depths of your evolution,
the changes and the chaos,
i promise to do the same with you.

through the pain

be brave enough
to love yourself
even when it hurts.

soft and whole

whatever you do, stay soft.
stay kind.

make room for yourself. stay whole.
stay gentle.

because the antics of
the world will make
you want to grow a shell
around your heart.

will make you feel
like all of you, as you
are, isn't enough to
be happy and live
fully.

whatever you do, stay soft.
stay kind.

make room for yourself. stay whole.
stay gentle.

well-meaning

meaning well and doing
well do not live in the
same house.

perhaps the two are neighbors.

but both cannot make a home
out of you, even if you let them.

contrast (ode to my younger self)

there is a difference, you know.

between need and want,
between love and lust.
between come and go,
forever and for now.

and yes, you will learn them all.
you will find their places on your
shelves,

one by one.

moving forward (after losing love)

there will be a next time.
and it may seemingly
dismantle you just like
the first.

but this time, you will
have the tools to put back
together the love you feel
like you lost.

careful

ease into yourself,
sweetly.

take your time.

there is no rush
to put yourself
back together
all at once.

transition

as the leaves dance
from their homes and
twirl to the ground.

as they perish and return
to the soft and forgiving soil

i remember that even at the end
of it all we can be just as beautiful
as the living.

choices

they don't have to come back.

and you don't have to answer

when they want to.

whirlwind

make room for disaster,
discovering, and damage,
because life isn't perfect.

sometimes it's a mess.

risk

have faith in your
ability to unfold.
trust your season
and bloom.
to open your heart
is to take a risk.

depth

everything that shatters us
creates room for self-discovery.
even in the thick of the mess
and madness lives magic.

with a wooden spoon

i scoop dried lavender
from the speckled clay
bowl that you gave me.

it still sits in the same spot
on the countertop.
and for a second
i fall in love so deeply
all over again.

the scent is pungent
but pleasant, light but
invigorating.

it reminds me of you
and what we could've
been

and why we aren't.

roar

unhappiness is loud.
and it can shatter every
bit of silence that gets
in the way

if you let it.

mosaic

make art with the mess
from your heart
on the floor.

adapt

one day you'll wake up
and everything will feel
different.

unlike it did before.

and you'll realize nothing, no matter
how you tilt it, will ever look the same.

forgive

freedom will sometimes
taste like forgiveness.

it may not always be
sweet, but it should be
savored.

darling

you will never
be small

with
a heart as big
as heaven

and a soul as
bright as neon.

Poem Prompts

—

These next few pages are for you to enjoy. Tap into your inner writer and create your own batch of poems. Get creative, have fun, and be bold and honest with your writing. This is your process! Write out your soul.

Write a poem using the following words:

Neon
Soul
Glow

Write a poem about healing and the process.

Write a haiku using these words:

Bloom
Curate
Unfold

Write a poem about your childhood and how it molded you.

Write a poem about flying without wings.

Write a poem about putting yourself first.

Write a poem about loss.

Write a poem about redemption.

Write a poem using these words:

Fray
Salt
Wash

Write an affirming letter to your younger or current self.

Index

—

ability, 91

adapt, 141

along the way, 37

autumn, 74

bad timing, 19

balance, 65

beautiful girl, 84

belong, 45

best friend, 60

blind, 113

bloom, 66

bogeyman, 76

bold, 36

boundaries, 28

brainwashed, 46

careful, 132

certainly, 112

choices, 134

clueless, 57

contrast
 (ode to my younger self), 130

creation, 122

credence, 108

daily, 59

daring, 35

darling, 143

death, 68

depth, 137

enjoy, 109

enjoy the journey, 110

escape, 10

evolution, 78

fill, 41

finale, 26

fine, 58

flight, 17

flow, 116

flowers, 31

fools have wings, 71

forgive, 142

freedom, 12

freedom, 101

from rejection, 93

gentleness, 115

grip, 38

hands, 42

healing, 62

hitchhiker, 33

homage, 119

how to birth a lesson, 77

husband, 96

impossible, 11

joy, 56

language, 80

learning alone, 94

light, 117

linger, 100

loose grip, 53

loss, 13

love lines, 18

masterpiece, 114

mercy, 30

mess, 21

miscarriage, 88

more than more, 125
   (ode to my daughter)

mosaic, 140

moving forward, 131
   (after losing love)

neon soul, 9

not for you, 82

one-sided, 79

opened door, 90

origin, 85

passage, 25

past life, 104

phoenix, 105

pieces, 40

push away, 24

real love, 73

rebirth, 52

refuge, 70

regret, 123

reminiscent of, 14

rescue, 99

resilience, 97

resilience practice, 63

revelation, 87

reward, 61

risk, 136

roar, 139

self-forgiveness, 29

self-love, 83

shame, 49

sixteen-year-old self, 64

soft and whole, 128

some is not all, 121

soul, 124

stay, 98

step by step, 111

stray, 54

student, 69

submit, 22

survive, 102

swallow falls, 32

tears, 34

the difference, 107

the journey to paper, 81

the one, 51

the ritual of healing, 20

the truth, 67

the unlearning, 44

through and through, 47

through the pain, 127

transition, 133

tutorial, 120

uncomfortable, 23

unconditional, 48

uncover, 106

uneasy, 92

unravel, 16

unseen, 39

upbringing, 27

uprising, 55

victim, 50

vigorous, 89

vows, 126

well-meaning, 129

when hearts break, 118

whirlwind, 135

whole, 15

whole, 72

wholeness, 103

with a wooden spoon, 138

write, 95

you, 86

Connect with Alex Elle
Instagram: @alex_elle
Twitter: @_alexelle
Website: alexelle.com

Andrews McMeel Publishing
a division of Andrews McMeel Universal
1130 Walnut Street, Kansas City, Missouri 64106

www.andrewsmcmeel.com

17 18 19 20 21 RR2 10 9 8 7 6 5 4 3 2

ISBN: 978-1-4494-8483-5

Library of Congress Control Number: 2016961724

Editor: Patty Rice
Creative Director: Tim Lynch
Designer: Laura Pol
Illustrator: Deun Ivory
Production Editor: Erika Kuster
Production Manager: Cliff Koehler

ATTENTION: SCHOOLS AND BUSINESSES

Andrews McMeel books are available at quantity discounts with bulk
purchase for educational, business, or sales promotional use. For information,
please e-mail the Andrews McMeel Publishing Special Sales Department:
specialsales@amuniversal.com.